ANCIENT SECRETS FOR KIDS

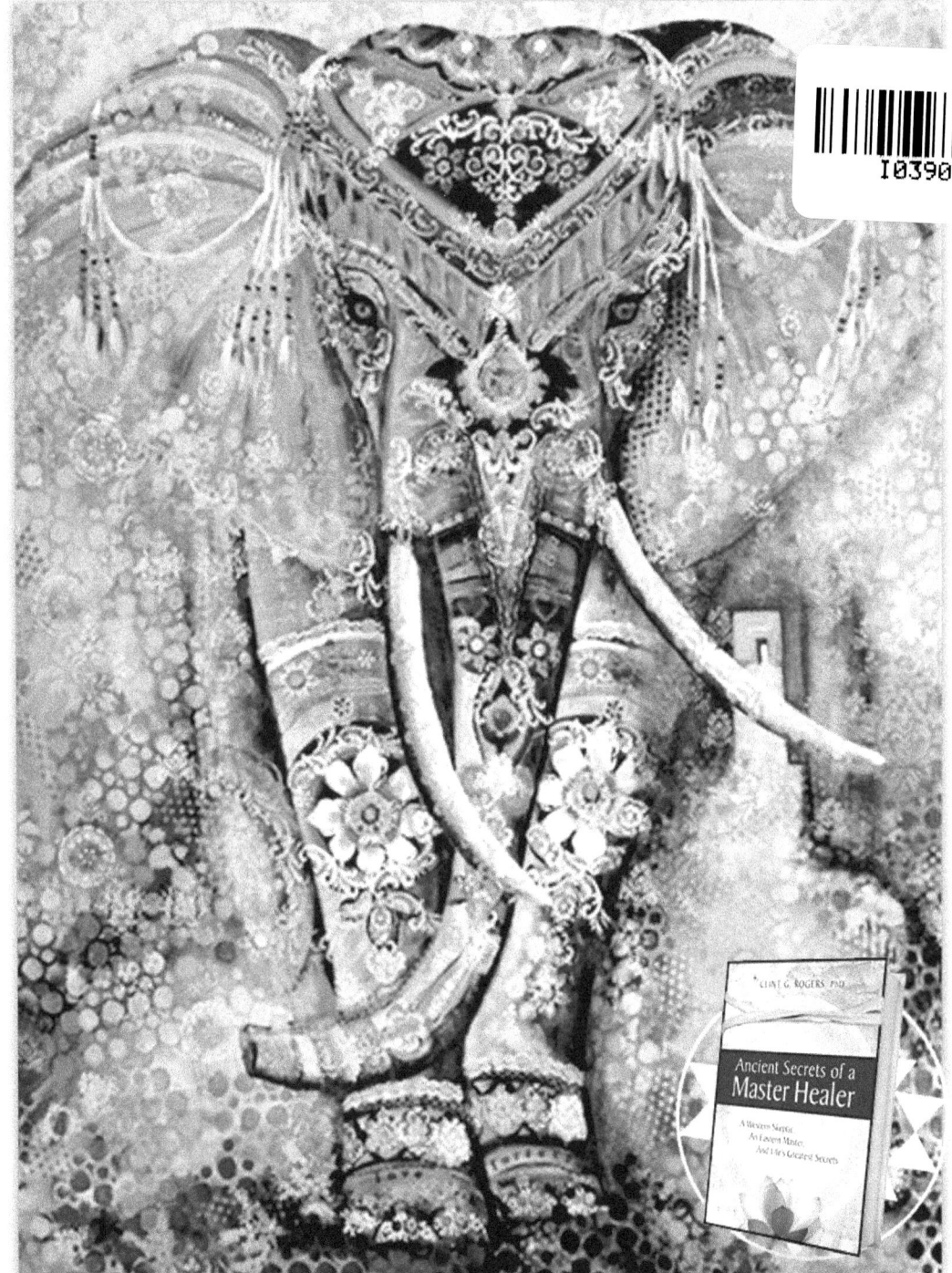

COLORING & ACTIVITY BOOK
Inspired by Dr. Naram, Dr. Clint G. Rogers,
and the book *Ancient Secrets of a Master Healer*

Copyright © 2022 by Wisdom of the World Press
Proceeds Benefit Ancient Secrets Foundation

Design & Content by: Dr. Clint G. Rogers & Heidi M. Aden

ISBN: 978-1-952353-99-4

All rights reserved.

No portion of this book may be reproduced in any form without written permission from the publisher or author, except as permitted by U.S. copyright law.

First printing edition 2022 in United States

www.MyAncientSecrets.com

THIS ART BOOK BELONGS TO:

Name:_____ Age:_____

WHO AM I?
Use the space below to draw yourself.

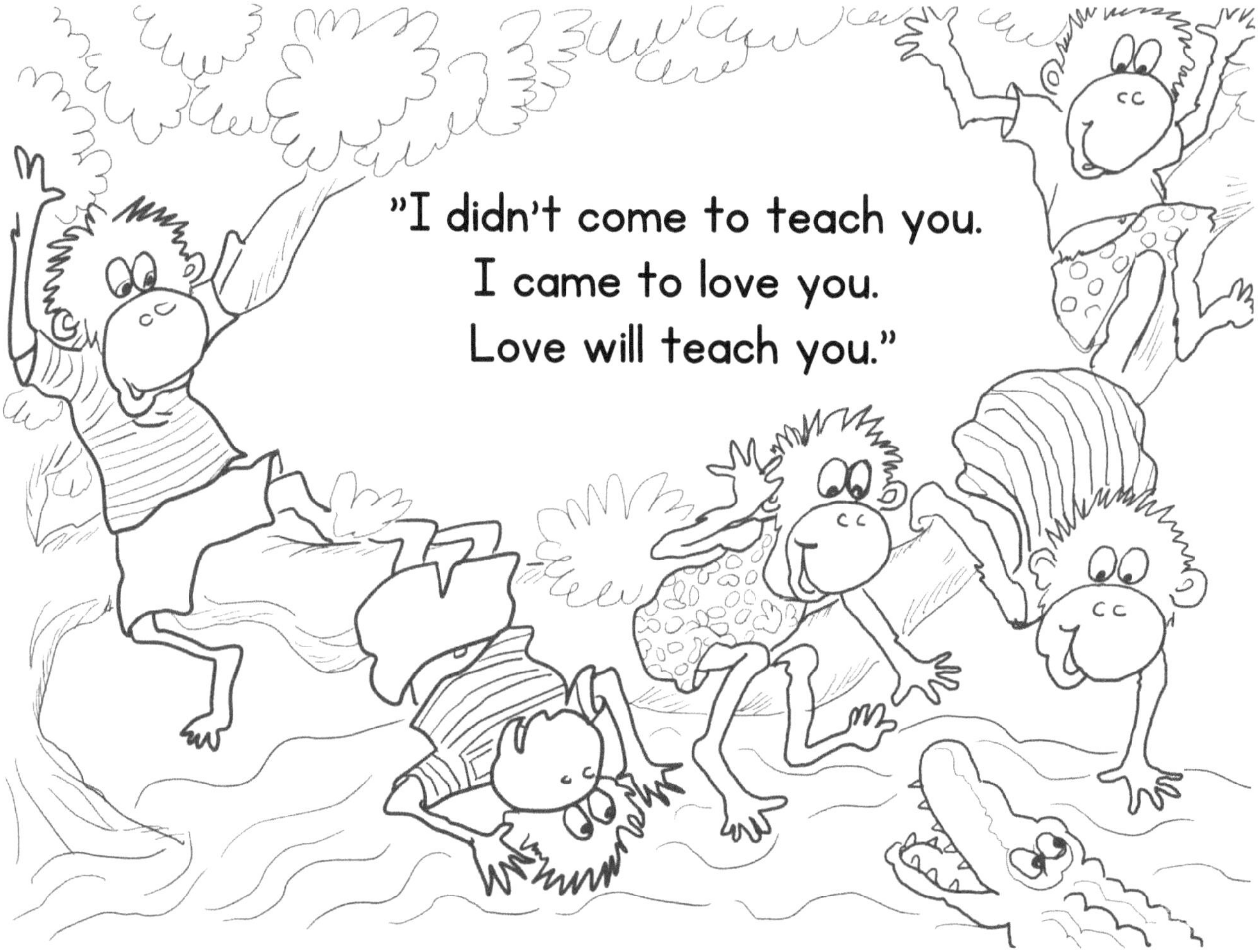
"I didn't come to teach you.
I came to love you.
Love will teach you."

Dr. Naram was a great healer who helped millions of people around the world by using Ancient Secrets from nature. Before he died, he passed on these secrets to his students, including Dr. Clint G. Rogers, who put many of them in a book called
'Ancient Secrets of a Master Healer'.

The book is being translated into over 30 languages so that people around the world can also learn these secrets for health and happiness.

Would you like to learn about Ancient Secrets for health and happiness?

In this coloring and activity book, you can learn many of these secrets, too!

Ancient Secrets of a Master Healer
Dr. Clint G. Rogers & Dr. Pankaj Naram

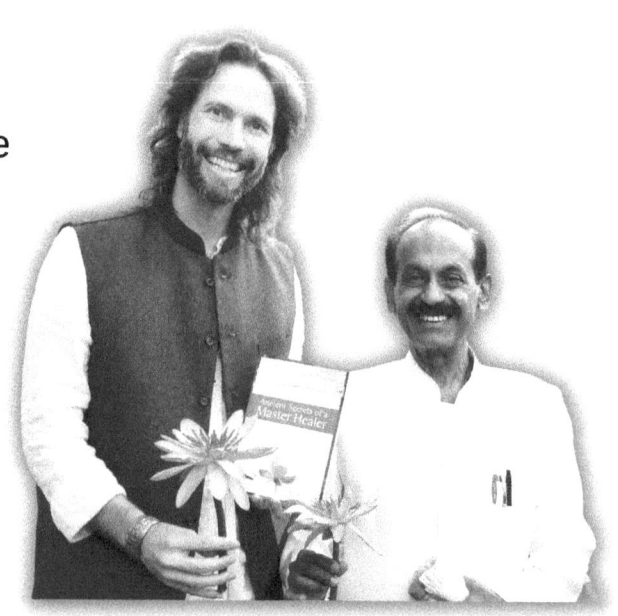

The Importance of knowing what you want

Dr. Naram's son, Krushna Naram, shares some wisdom his father passed on to him many times throughout the years.

One of the most important things to help you achieve a healthy balanced life is to know what you want.

Ancient Secrets of a Master Healer (ASMH), **page 6**

Dr. Naram & Krushna Naram

WHAT DO YOU WANT?

1)

2)

3)

What do you want . . .
to be a paleontologist and study fossils?
(A paleontologist is a scientist who studies fossils and the remains of ancient organisms.)

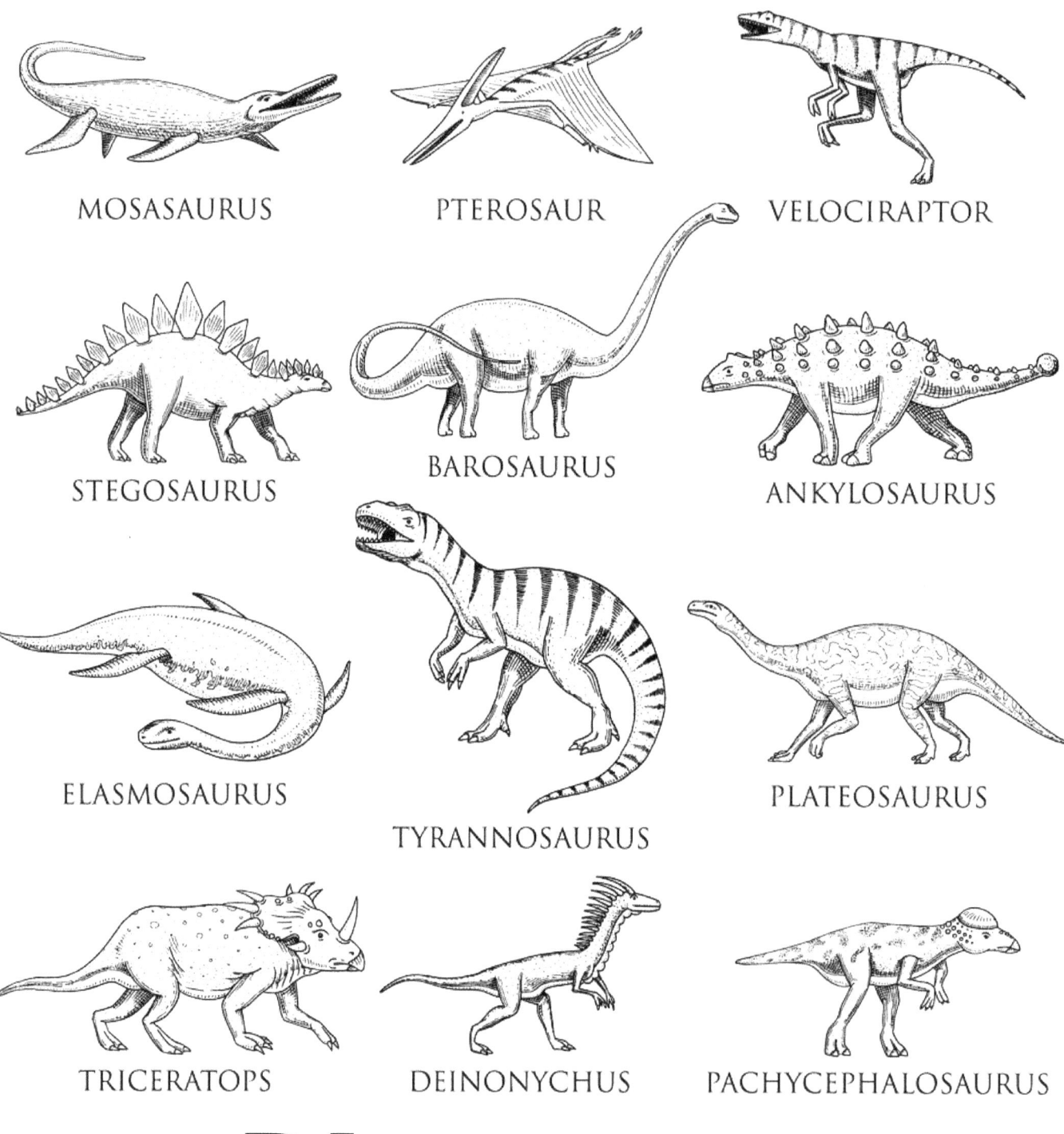

Dinosaurs

Tyrannosaurus rex

Brachiosaurus

A Gift From the Heart...

When these two boys from Germany found out about the orphan kids in need, they had a big desire to help. Yes, they decided to give their own money to help support them, but also donated their awesome dinosaur collection! In doing so, they inspired many other adults and children to give from their hearts. Dr. Naram and Dr. Clint had the honor of delivering the dinosaurs to the orphan kids in Nepal, and with them, all of the love from these two boys. Many more were inspired to give when they heard about their actions. It's amazing what can happen when you let love guide you!

Jonathan & George Simon (middle) with their mother, Dr. Naram, Dr. Clint, and their father.

Dr. Naram and some of the Orphans sharing and playing with the dinosaurs donated by Jonathan & George Simon.
Ancient Secrets Foundation helps orphans like these all over the world.

Sea Turtle

The oldest known sea turtle fossil is at least 120 million years old. That means they shared the planet with dinosaurs which became extinct around 65 million years ago.

What do you want . . .
to be an astronaut and explore the universe?

Astronaut

What do you want . . .
to be a singer or a musician?

Music

"Music is life. That's why our hearts have beats." - Cecily Morgan

What do you want . . .
to be a veterinarian and take care of animals?

Did you know...

Ancient Secrets works on humans, animals, and plants too!

ASMH, page 187

Master Healer, Dr. Pankaj Naram pulse healing with the elephant Laxmi, the gentle giant.

Did you know?
Elephants are excellent swimmers and can hear through their feet.

Master healer, Dr. Pankaj Naram pulse healing with a royal bengal tiger.

Did you know?

Tigers are very adaptable and smart animals with one of the longest short-term memories among all animals, including humans.

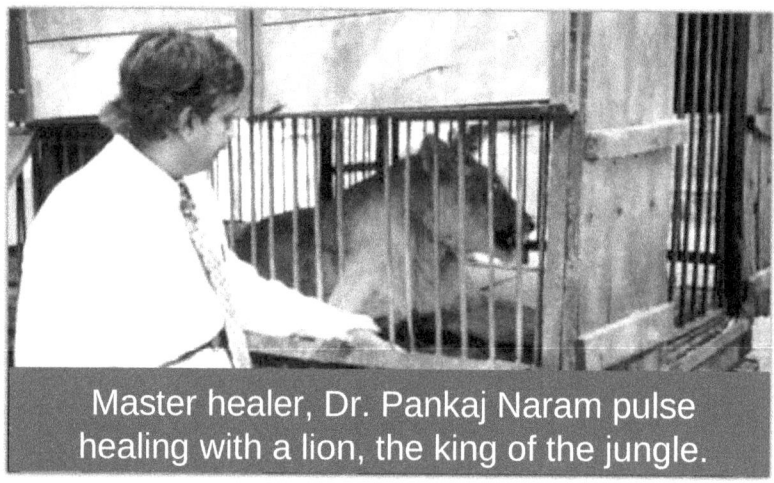

Master healer, Dr. Pankaj Naram pulse healing with a lion, the king of the jungle.

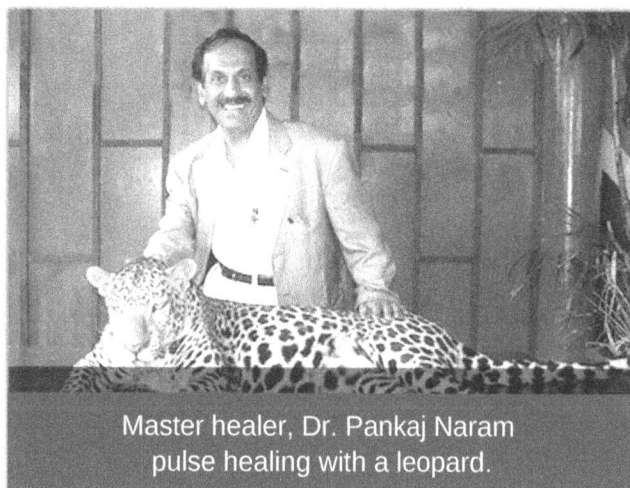

Master healer, Dr. Pankaj Naram pulse healing with a leopard.

Dr. Naram pulse healing and giving home remedies for wounds to a giant python.

Tiger

Tigers are the largest cat species in the world, reaching up to 3.3 meters (almost 11 feet) in length and weighing up to 670 pounds!

Lion

African lions have been admired throughout history as symbols of courage and strength.

Dr. Giovanni Brincivalli
To The Rescue!

Dr. Naram & Dr. Giovanni

Dr. Giovanni is one of Dr. Naram's lifelong friends and colleagues. One day, Dr. Giovanni was called by a beekeeper who had sick bees. A destructive parasite infected the bees with a virus and they stopped producing honey and started to die.

Dr. Giovanni did some research and learned this type of infection makes the bees weak, they don't fly and some lose all their body hair. Dr. Giovanni recalled Dr. Naram treating patients with Ancient Secrets remedies for immunity and hair loss. He and the beekeeper crushed some of Dr. Naram's herbs, mixed it with honey, and fed it to the bees. A short time later the beekeeper called Dr. Giovanni and said the bees were growing their hair back and were looking healthier and stronger.

ASMH, **page 187**

The reason bees are so noisy is because they beat their wings 11,400 times in one minute!

Help the beekeeper get to the beehive

Use your imagination to decorate the honeycomb with your favorite colors and designs.

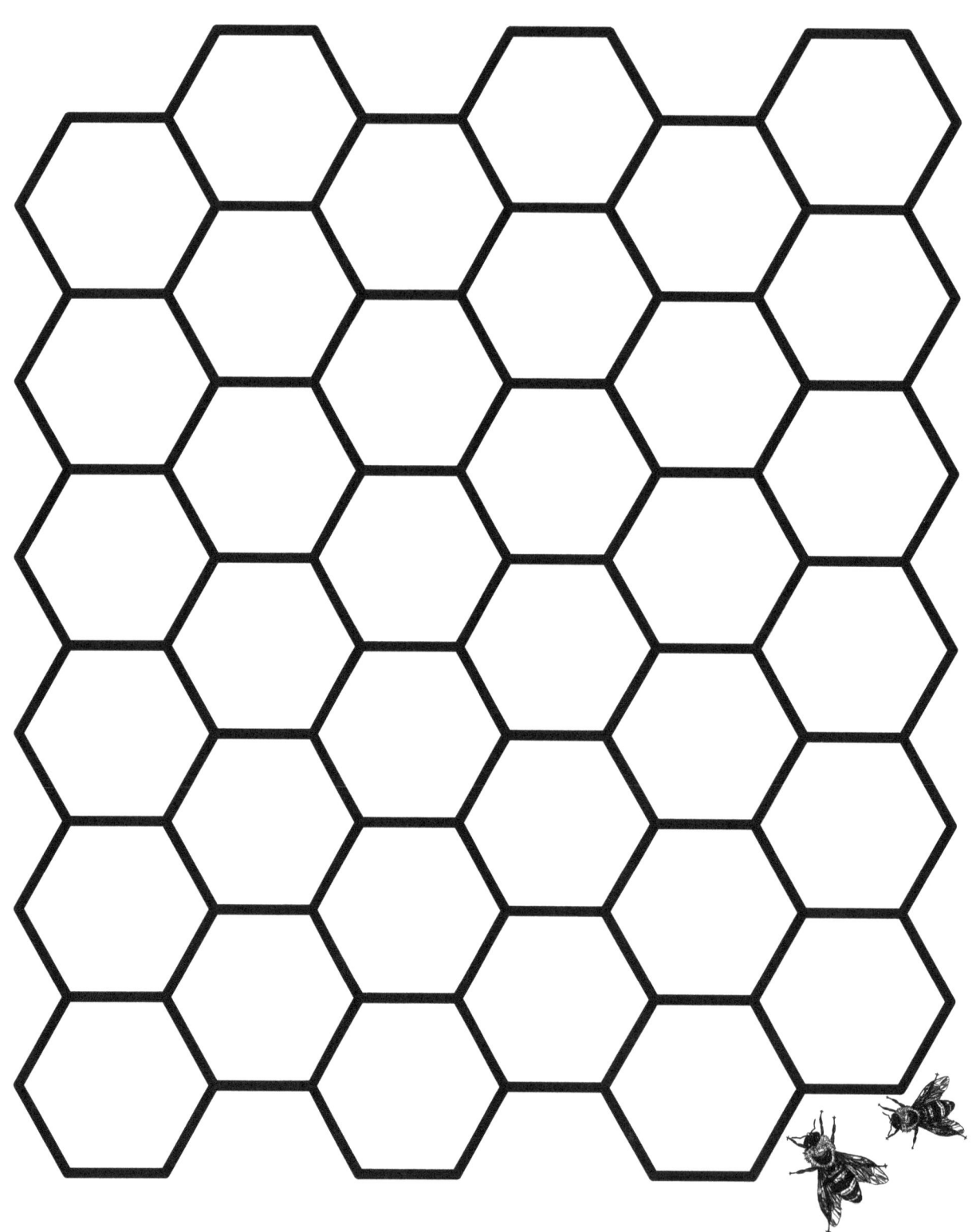

Ancient healing secrets work on humans, animals, and plants too! But how?

ASMH, page 189

Dr. Naram said there are 6 Secret Keys of Siddha-Veda:

1) Diet
2) Herbal Formulas
3) Home Remedies
4) Marmaa Shakti
5) Lifestyle
6) Panchkarma or Asthakarma

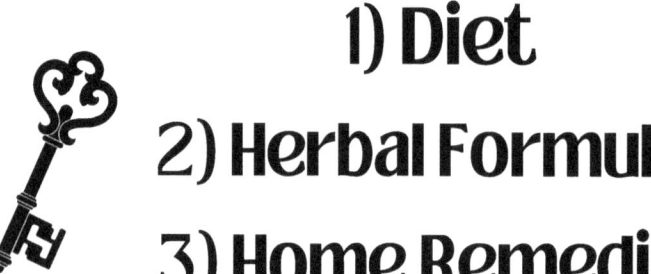

"Siddha-Veda has six secret keys of deeper healing, which can transform anyone's body, mind, and emotions." - Dr. Naram

Ancient Secrets Key 1: Diet

"Everything can be either a poison or a medicine, depending on how you use it."

- Jivaka
(Ancient Physician of Buddha)

Diet - what you eat and what you avoid eating can help keep you healthy & happy.

What's your favorite fruit?

"If you change your food, you can change your future." - Dr. Naram

Miraculous Moong Bean Soup

Moong soup is one of many powerful tools shared by Dr. Naram and the book 'Ancient Secrets of a Master Healer'.

Why Eat Moong Soup?

Moong Beans are an amazing food! Your body benefits in many ways when you eat this SOUP-er food:

- Helps to balance all body types (all 3 doshas: Vata, Pitta & Kapha)
- Helps clear away the things that build up inside, clogging our bodies (called toxins, or 'aam').
- Helps your body heal with SOUP-er speed! (Especially with cooked green vegetables.)
- Power-paced with vitamins, minerals, and protein (one of the best plant-based sources!)
- So many other incredible benefits - your body will love you for it!

Dr. Naram's Moong Bean Soup Recipe is included at the end of this book!

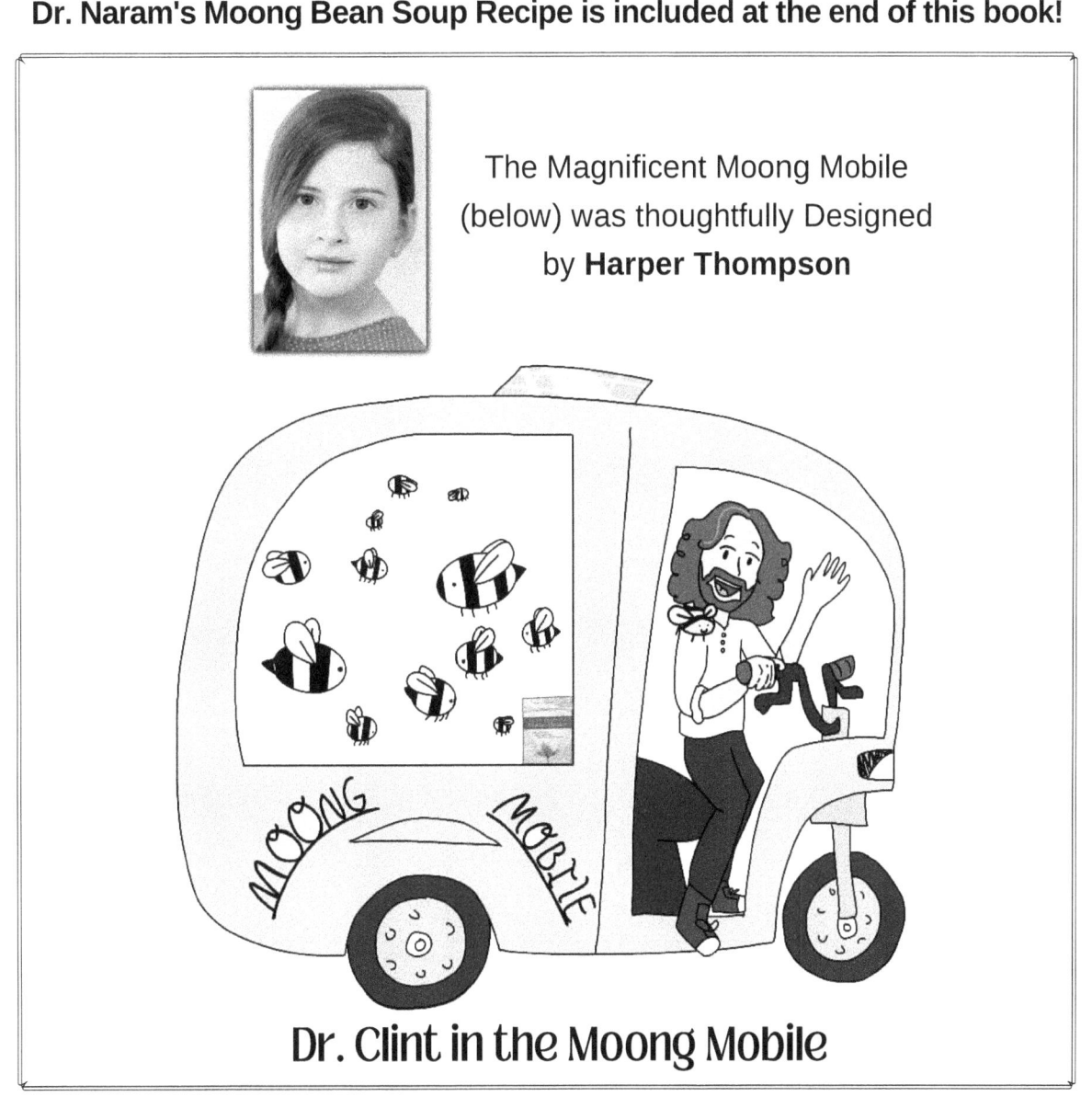

The Magnificent Moong Mobile (below) was thoughtfully Designed by **Harper Thompson**

Dr. Clint in the Moong Mobile

Moong Bean Nutritional Information

One cup (7 ounces or 202 grams) of boiled moong beans contains (reference):

Calories: 212
Fat: 0.8 grams
Protein: 14.2 grams
Carbs: 38.7 grams
Fiber: 15.4 grams
Folate (B9): 80% of the Reference Daily Intake (RDI)
Manganese: 30% of the RDI
Magnesium: 24% of the RDI
Vitamin B1: 22% of the RDI
Phosphorus: 20% of the RDI
Iron: 16% of the RDI
Copper: 16% of the RDI
Potassium: 15% of the RDI
Zinc: 11% of the RDI
Vitamins B2, B3, B5, B6 and selenium

Moong Bean Soup ©
Artwork by **Maryam Khalifah**

MaryamArtIllustration.com

I didn't come to teach you. I came to love you. Love will teach you. - DR. Pankaj Naram

Ancient Secrets Key 2: Herbal Formulas

Herbal Formulas - these formulas are made from plants and spices that the ancient masters knew how to mix and use to help people. These herbal formulas still work today and help us stay healthy or help us get better when we are sick.

Ancient Secrets Key 3: Home Remedies

Can the Ancient Secrets that helped
the bees help you, too?

Some of the best remedies can be mixed in your own kitchen. Here is the Ancient Secrets Home Remedy that can help boost your immunity so that you get sick less and recover more quickly.

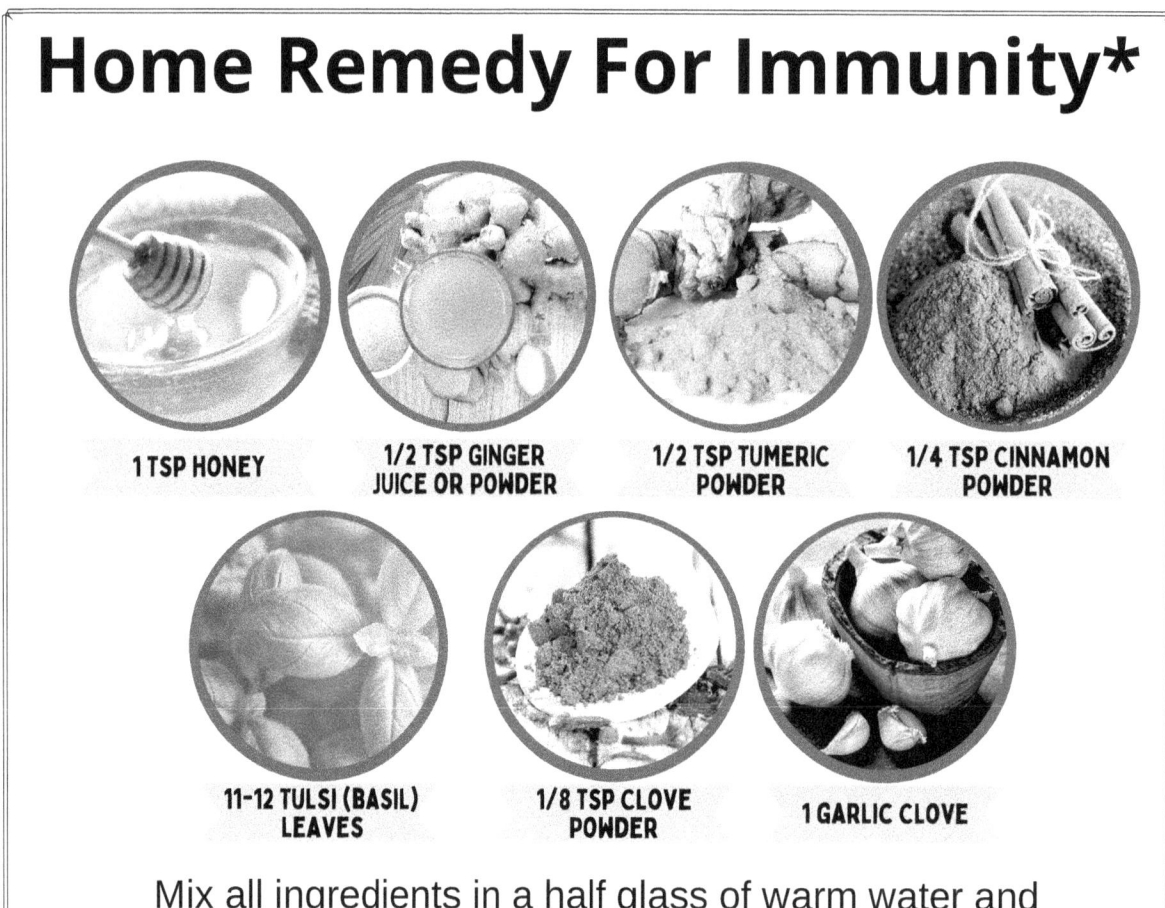

*Notes:
- The garlic clove is optional (if for religious reasons you avoid garlic, then you don't need to include it).
- Some recommend not to give babies under 1 year old honey.
- Please read the medical disclaimer on the last page

Ancient Secrets Key 4: Marmaa Shakti

The ancient masters knew about energy points on the body. When these points are pressed, they can help you in different ways.

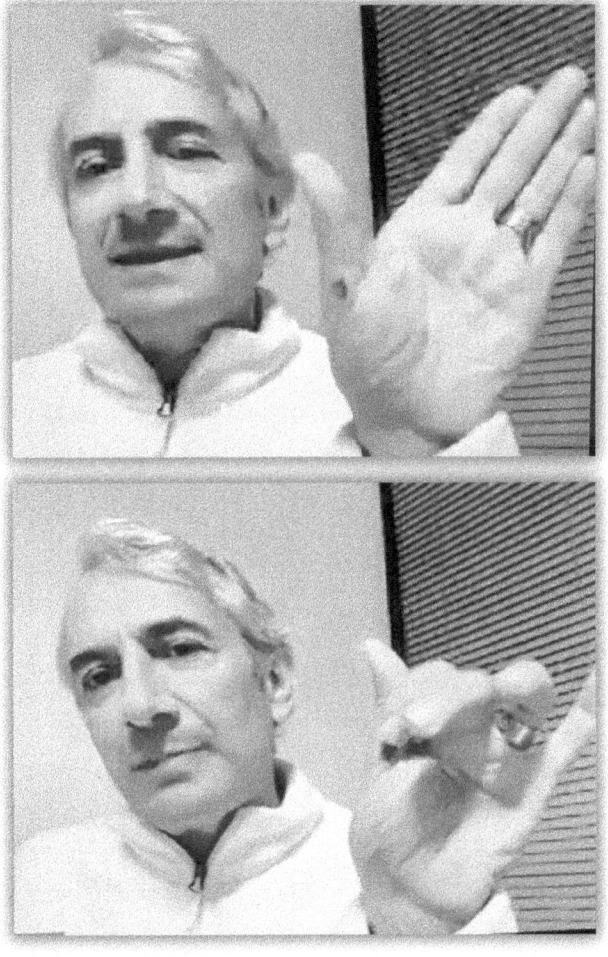

Photo 1

Photo 2

Dr. Giovanni shares the Marmaa Shakti point to Boost Memory & Concentration

In photo 1: Notice the dot on Dr. Giovanni's left thumb - this is the point you want to press firmly.

In photo 2: Fold your first finger on your left hand down and press this point firmly 6 times. Do this 6 times throughout the day.

*To discover many Marmaa Shakti points that can help with various things, see **'Ancient Secrets of a Master Healer'**

Ancient Secrets Key 5: Lifestyle

Taking time to exercise, sleep properly, meditate and/or pray, and even who you choose to be your friends can have an impact on your health and happiness.

Take time to meditate - it helps balance your body, mind, and soul.

Ancient Secrets Key 6: Panchkarma or Asthakarma

PANCHKARMA is an ancient process that takes several weeks and involves nutritional changes, massages, and more. This process can help clean one's body of toxins, and can help to feel more healthy and energetic.

One Ancient Secret is to practice 'Atithi Devo Bhava'

Atithi Devo Bhava

means "treat an unexpected guest as if God (himself or herself) has come to visit you".

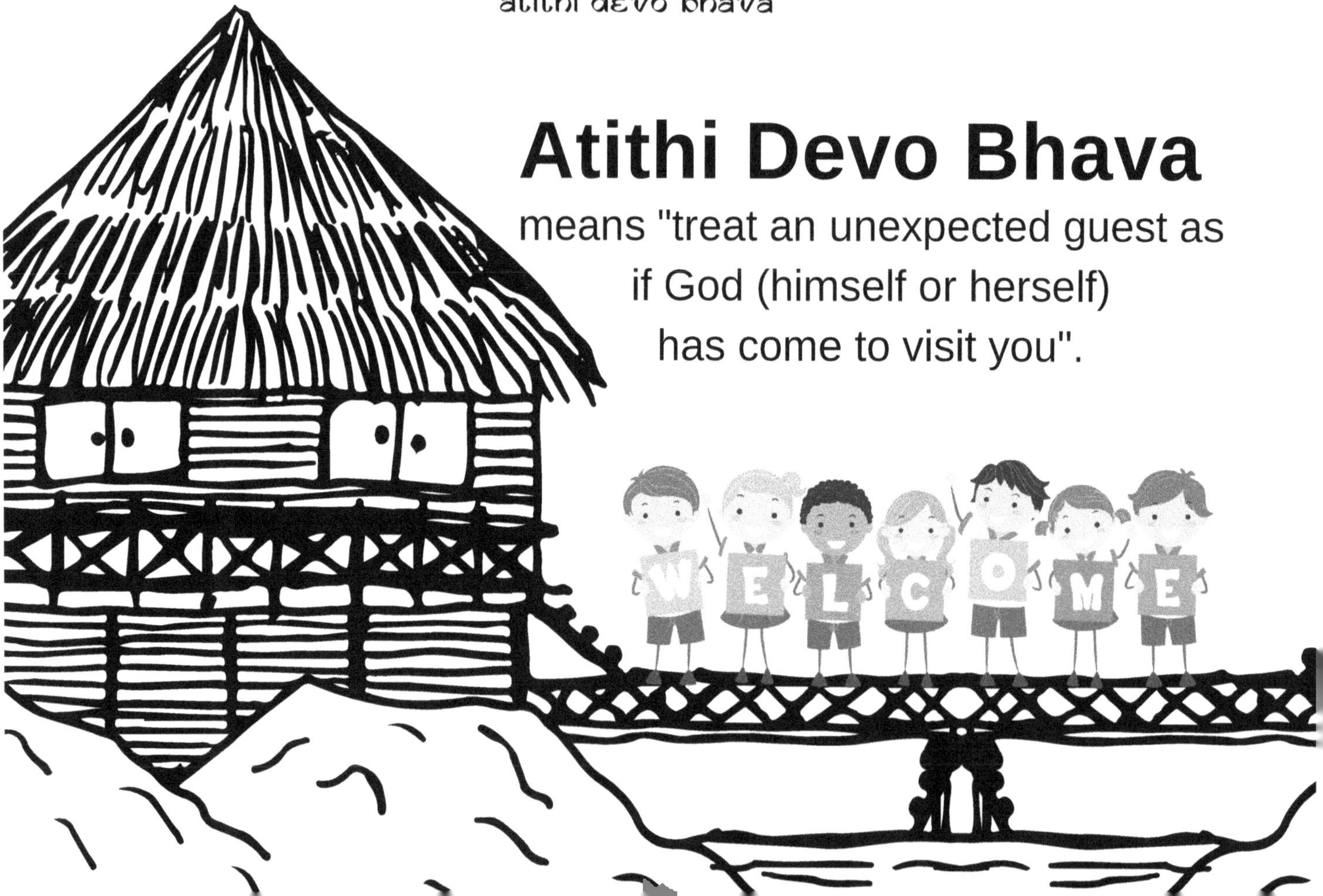

Dr. Clint & Milo

Sometimes an "unexpected guest" can come in the form of a challenge that arrives into our lives.

For Dr. Clint one challenge was when Dr. Naram passed on, and he was feeling very lonely. The morning after the Dr. Naram's prayer service, Dr. Clint was walking the streets of Mumbai, very sad. Suddenly a dog showed up that wouldn't leave his side. They soon became best friends and this dog, Milo, reminded Dr. Clint that we are never alone, and that miracles do happen. This is how they started "The Miracle Experiment Game" together. Now people all over the world can play together to see miracles happen in their lives by applying these Ancient Secrets. *ASMH,* page 274

What is one 'unexpected guest' or challenge that has come into your life which ended up being a gift?

Dogs

Just like people, dogs come in all shapes and sizes - each one is unique and special, just like you!

As part of the Miracle Experiment Game, Dr. Clint asks people to go out of their way to feed animals (especially dogs, cows, and crows).

Cows are the favorite animal in many countries; they serve as a symbol of wealth, strength, and abundance.

What is most important in life?

Dr. Naram says 3 of the most important things are:

- to know what you want,
- to achieve what you want,
- and to enjoy what you achieve.

The Ancient Secrets can help you to do all three.

ASMH, page 216

"In the last 6 thousand years of human history, the greatest need people have is not love, but understanding." -Baba Ramdas (Dr. Naram's Master)

ASMH, page 72

Art by Paras Aggarwal, age 14

WHAT IS ANOTHER ANCIENT SECRET TO BE HAPPY?

•GRATITUDE•

List 3 things you are grateful for:

1)

2)

3)

List 3 things that make you happy:

1)

2)

3)

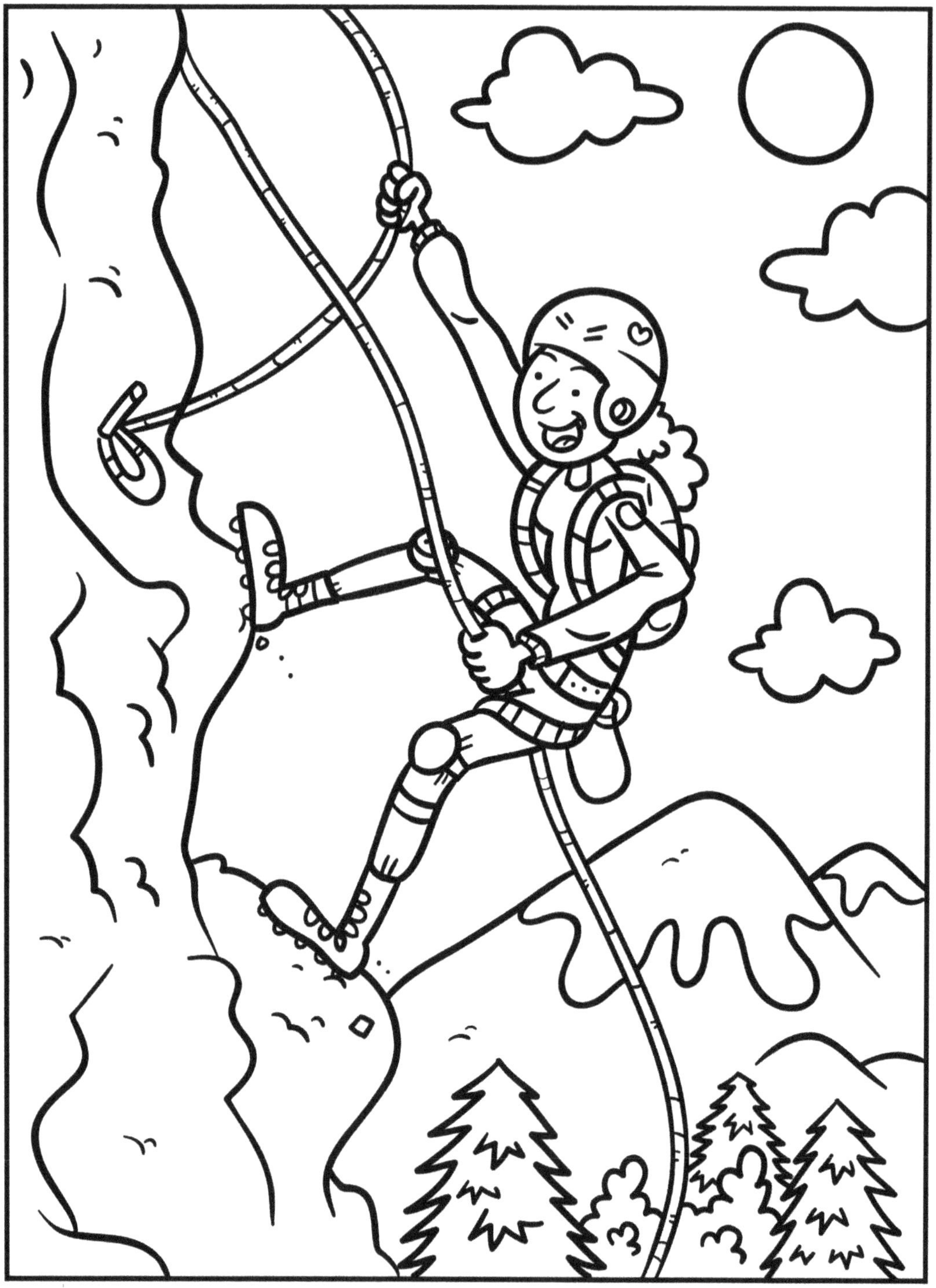

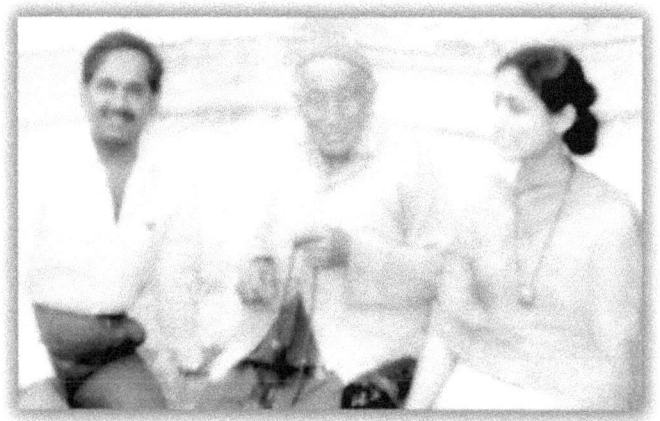

Dr. Pankaj & Smita Naram with Baba Ramdas

"No matter how big the problem or difficulty, never give up hope!"

- B*aba Ramdas*
(Dr. Naram's Master)
***ASMH*, page 4**

Lotus Flower

"My master said just as the brilliant white lotus flower rises out of the dark mud to share its brightness and fragrance with us all, so must these ancient healing secrets open up to reveal their deeper healing beauty with all humanity. It is simply a school of thought that anyone can join and benefit from – by learning how to help themselves and others heal deeper and deeper." - Dr. Naram

ASMH, page 252

Tree of Life

Ancient Secrets Foundation has a mission to help and protect animals, trees, orphans, plants, and all of life.

These wonderful orphans from Nepal are making bracelets to show their support for people that were affected by the earthquake.

Ancient Secrets Foundation helps support kids like these with necessary elements like shoes and clothing, educational materials, love and support.

Denny & Gill

Denny and Gill grew up in orphanages and later became great friends. Together they discovered that LOVE can overcome any challenge! Find out more about how they inspire people around the world in the new book, *'Love is the Only Truth'*.

Our beloved Gill tossing hats she made with love for the orphans of Nepal.

"Make your work like a prayer. Doing work you love keeps you feeling young, no matter your age." - Dr. Naram

ASMH, page 80

"God is within each of us, and we all have a purpose to discover." - Baba Ramdas (Dr. Naram's Master)

Dr. Naram's Mission: "To bring the benefit of Ancient Secrets into every home, and every heart on earth."
Draw your vision of a happy earth.

Dr. Smita Naram, Dr. Pankaj Naram & son Krushna Naram

Dr. Clint, Dr. Naram & Milo

To go deeper into the Ancient Secrets you can visit: MyAncientSecrets.com

Dr. Naram's Marvelous Moong Bean Soup Recipe

Once you make this basic recipe, you can then experiment with some slight alterations, to master the perfect recipe for you.

(Note: It is very important to read labels on any spices and other products you may want to add, in order to avoid preservatives and extra processed foods. They should be gluten free, dairy free, and contained no refined sugars)

Ingredients

- 1 Cup Whole Green Dried Moong Beans
- 2 Cups Water + 1-1/2 TSP Salt
- 1 TBSP Cow's Ghee or Sunflower Oil
- 1 TSP Black Mustard Seeds
- 2 Pinches Hing (also called Asafoetida)
- 1 Bay Leaf
- 1/2 TSP Turmeric Powder
- 1 TSP Cumin Powder
- 1 TSP Coriander Powder
- 1 Pinch Black Pepper
- 1-1/2 TSP Fresh Ginger, finely chopped or Ground Ginger
- 1/2-1 TSP or 1 Clove Fresh Garlic, finely chopped or Garlic Powder
- 2 more cups of water - add to make soup after beans are cooked
- 3 Pieces of Kokum (dry jungle plum)
- Salt to taste when served
- Optional: 1 Cup peeled chopped Carrots; 1 Cup diced Celery

Preparation Steps

1. Rinse, remove any debris, and then soak the moong beans in water overnight. (Add 1 tsp baking soda while it soaks to help reduce gas.)
2. Drain and rinse the moong beans, adding the indicated amount of water and salt, then cook in a pressure cooker until tender. It takes around 25 minutes, depending on your pressure cooker. (The beans have to be broken.)
3. Or, in a regular deep pot, it will take 40-45 minutes for the beans to be fully cooked. Bring to a boil then to low heat with the lid on or cracked slightly. Add Kokum, carrots and celery after 25 minutes.
4. While beans are cooking, after about 20 minutes, heat the oil or ghee in a separate deep pot on medium heat until melted. Add mustard seeds.
5. When the seeds start to pop, add the hing, bay leaf, turmeric, cumin, coriander, ginger, garlic, and a pinch of black pepper and stir gently, mixing well.
6. Quickly turn heat to lowest setting. Simmer about 10 minutes — do not allow to burn.
7. Transfer the cooked beans with 2 more cups fresh water into the pot with the simmering ingredients.
8. Bring to a boil then simmer 5-10 minutes more. Enjoy! Can be served with basmati rice.

Recipe from: Ancient Secrets of a Master Healer

**Discover videos on how to make this soup, plus other recipes and more on:
MyAncientSecrets.com**

How Can You Discover More Ancient Secrets?

 Important Links and Contact Info:

To get your copy of 'Ancient Secrets of a Master Healer' and join the community or any of our courses visit: MyAncientSecrets.com

Classes & Education:

100-Day Ancient Secrets Training

Discover and apply specific ancient healing secrets in your own life. Learn more about the basics of Ayurveda/Siddha-Veda. This learning experience is packed with educational videos, home remedies, marmaas, and much more!

30-Day Miracle Experiment Experience

Now in English, Spanish, Russian, and Italian! Unlock Your Ancient Secret Power. Experience more vibrant health, unlimited energy, and peace of mind. A fun, interactive experience in a group setting.

Plus More! Please see MyAncientSecrets.com

  Community:

Free Global Miracle Call Every Sunday

Join us live on zoom or on Dr Clint's FaceBook page each Sunday.
Time: 8AM Pacific / 11AM Eastern

Ancient Secrets Foundation

Proceeds from this book benefit orphan kids in Nepal and important projects helping Ancient Secrets to benefit people around the world. If you feel inspired to volunteer or support us in any way please fill out the form to join the Miracle Dream Team on: www.MyAncientSecrets.com
Or email us at: team@MyAncientSecrets.com

 *Disclaimer:

*All content was created for informational purposes only. The content is not intended to be a substitute for professional medical advice, diagnosis, or treatment. Always seek the advice of your physician or other qualified health provider with any questions you may have regarding a medical condition. Never disregard professional medical advice or delay in seeking it because of something you have read in this book.

We hope that you enjoyed this version of Ancient Secrets for Kids Coloring & Activity Book!

www.ingramcontent.com/pod-product-compliance
Lightning Source LLC
Chambersburg PA
CBHW051400110526
44592CB00023B/2897